The Hero of Skid Row

George Mitchell

Bloomington, IN  Milton Keynes, UK

AuthorHouse™
1663 Liberty Drive, Suite 200
Bloomington, IN 47403
www.authorhouse.com
Phone: 1-800-839-8640

AuthorHouse™ UK Ltd.
500 Avebury Boulevard
Central Milton Keynes, MK9 2BE
www.authorhouse.co.uk
Phone: 08001974150

This book is a work of fiction. People, places, events, and situations are the product of the author's imagination. Any resemblance to actual persons, living or dead, or historical events, is purely coincidental.

© 2006 George Mitchell. All rights reserved.

No part of this book may be reproduced, stored in a retrieval system, or transmitted by any means without the written permission of the author.

First published by AuthorHouse 9/14/2006

ISBN: 1-4259-3682-2 (sc)

Printed in the United States of America
Bloomington, Indiana

This book is printed on acid-free paper.

This book is dedicated to every person that refused to accept skid row as their home and found the courage to walk away and climb the ladder to success.

THE HERO OF SKID ROW

The back of our truck was being loaded with the finest cow manure the Chicago Stock Yards had to offer. The powerful stench guaranteed that our vegetables would grow bigger, our grass would grow greener, and our berries would be sweeter than the other farmers around us. That was our reason for making five trips a week from Michigan to Illinois early in the spring.

Smoke was rising from top of our smelly cargo as we drove away from the yards. We stopped at a traffic light and a man wearing very tattered clothing climbed up onto the running board and asked for money. My dad gave him a couple of dollars.

George Mitchell

Another man saw what had happened and ran over to our truck. This time my dad shook his head and the man blasted us with his entire vocabulary of vulgarity. He sure knew a lot of curse words.

The light changed and my dad started to drive ahead, but the raggedy man with the potty mouth still wasn't finished with us. He ended the one way conversation by pulling down his pants and mooning us as we drove away.

I thought that was the funniest thing I had ever seen and had myself a good laugh. Without changing his expression my dad said to me, "Don't laugh at them".

My dad was a man few words and I knew he had finished talking about it unless I asked the question, so I asked. "Who was those people and why were they carrying those dirty blankets and sleeping on the ground"? "Why were they acting like that"?

He used a few words that said a lot. "They made bad choices". "Life is filled with good and bad possibilities". "The choices we make in life can cause us to become heroes or zeroes".

That conversation was over, but a seed had been planted in my mind that would grow into a life time goal. "Be a hero". "Don't let myself become a Zero".

Growing up on a farm in south western Michigan was a good life but it didn't prepare me for the treachery of life beyond the boundaries of the homestead. My parents used words from the bible to help shape my character and I memorized the "Ten Commandments" to help me stay focused.

High school was easy and like most other kids my favorite subjects were lunch and recess. Basketball was my first love and everyone knew I was the best shooter on the team except the coach. I tried my best to elevate myself to "hero" status there, but the coach wasn't about to let that happen.

He would put me in the game when my team was behind. If I managed to bring the team back and put them in a position to win the game with the last shot, the coach would immediately call time out, and replace me with the same person I had replaced. They would run a play to get him the last shot and we would ride home with long faces again. I hated that.

I never understand his logic, or why he totally overlooked me when he was trying to create a hero. Rejection was hard to accept when I knew I was the one he was searching for.

I was watching as the school buses pulled in and parked that monday morning. This was the day that kids from other areas were being bussed to our school for the first time. She stepped off the bus and stole my heart.

She walked with her head held high and her chest stuck out. She passed close to me and blew me away with a smile. I didn't need any help figuring it out "I was in love". I found out later from her sister that her name was Geraldine.

Graduating from high school was the first real goal I set for myself. The Marine Corps recruiter made it real easy for me to set the next one. He used the word "hero" during the first minute of our meeting. I didn't hear the rest of his speech. I was going to be a "Hero".

Corporal Kerr was the first person to make me doubt my sanity when we got off the bus in San Diego. He stood about six foot seven inches tall, had a very deep voice and shoulders so wide the back pack he wore looked like a match box in the middle of his back. When he opened his mouth we kind of expected thunder to come out. He wasn't a man, "He was a marine".

I didn't know there were grown men in this world that couldn't do a push-up, or pull up, or sit up before I got to boot camp. There were even guys that couldn't run a block. I wondered what it would be like for a drill instructor to have a whole platoon of guys like that.

Three years later I returned to M.C.R.D. San Diego as a drill instructor and was faced with finding the answer to that question.

They were the worst looking group of marine rejects I had ever seen. I didn't even want to attempt making marines out of them until someone mentioned that the guy that could make marines out of this motley looking crew would be a real "hero".

I did such a good job with my platoon that half of them were promoted when they graduated from Boot Camp. My commanding officer was even promoted.

My name appeared on the printed program but was misspelled. How can anyone misspell "George"? I began to feel that someone up there hated me.

I was transferred to the "hand-to-hand combat" section, but that didn't work out very well. They said I had some pent up hostility because I had a hard time pulling punches and bloodied some noses, blacked some eyes, dislocated some knee caps and broke a few bones.

Behind my back they nicknamed me "Devil Dog", and began to play sick to keep from training with me.

I spent eleven years two months and fourteen days putting forth the effort, but was always overlooked when the word "promotion" or "hero" was mentioned.

I tried to overlook it at first when the men I trained were promoted ahead of me. I would then train new men and watch as they were also promoted. I hadn't been promoted in six years. I might as well have been invisible.

Some of the men I trained were now two stripes ahead of me. I had spent two tours away from the United States. One of those tours was in a combat zone. No one seemed to notice or care. I remember thinking to myself, "It didn't take Deputy Dawg this long to become a hero".

I had transformed men that couldn't do a sit up push up, or pull up into competent combat ready marines,

The Hero of Skid Row

I pushed and pulled men that couldn't run a block into men that could run all day if the wanted to.

I had made sharpshooters out of men that were afraid of guns. I had taught cowards to watch each other's back. I had taught men to be proud of the uniform they wore, but I never became the hero I set out to be.

I was honorably discharged after Viet Nam, but the idea that I was destined to be a "hero" was rapidly fading into obscurity.

I returned to Michigan and went to work for the postal service. I transferred to Las Vegas as soon as the opportunity presented itself. When I arrived in Las Vegas I was informed that there was a hiring freeze and I didn't have a job.

Las Vegas was constant motion, bright lights and instant slot machine addiction. It's very easy to get caught up in the allusion of getting rich by winning, "The Big One".

I was down to my last twenty dollars when the panic attack arrived. Two hours ago I had more than seven hundred dollars. I now had twenty.

My car was still in the parking lot filled with all of my stuff. I didn't have a place to stay. I couldn't afford a room, and I didn't know anyone. I felt like standing by the door and asking everyone that came in to kick my butt.

That was not an option because I would have to leave the machine to do that. I wasn't about to do that because all of my money was in there. I took a deep breath and reluctantly dropped three coins in and pulled the handle.

Bright lights began to flash. Bells began to ring and three red sevens stared back at me. I had just won a thousand dollars

"Yeah Buddy". That's when the word "hero" was replaced by the word "winner". I could live with that.

I collected my money and found myself an apartment. I had found out real quick how foolish a country boy could be when the bells are ringing and the lights are flashing all around him. Three days later I started working at that casino.

I stayed in Las Vegas two years. During that time I started three different businesses that failed. I finally realized that I could not prosper with slot machines around me.

I completed another business plan that really had a chance if I started it some place else. My life as a gambler had been a good example of a "zero". I intended to take another shot at becoming a "hero". I packed up my stuff and drove to Los Angeles. Everything went down hill from there.

I had a flat tire on the south side of Los Angeles. It was dusk dark and I could see the gas station ahead. I really didn like the way the neighborhood looked, so I decided to put a can of "fix a flat" in the tire and drive to the station and get the flat tire fixed while I put the spare tire on the car. It seemed like a good idea to me.

1 locked the car and left my emergency flashers blinking. I quickly jogged to the station and back. I came back to a car that had been trashed.

My stuff had been scattered on the ground, the trunk had been pried open and everything worth anything was gone. I walked back to the station feeling like a loser.

I made friends with the son of a preacher at the station. He offered me a place to stay for a modest fee. My money went faster than expected.

George Mitchell

We worked temporary assignments that took us nowhere. I decided that this was not the life I wanted and walked all the way down town. I really needed to rest. The bus stop up ahead looked pretty good to me.

THE WITNESS

The gold trimmed black Mercedes moved at a snails pace down Sixth Street. The Attorney behind the wheel reeked of success and confidence. He was the one you wanted on your side in a court room. He appeared to be unshakable.

The curvaceous blonde on the passenger side was wearing a low cut blouse that partially exposed the most attractive decorations to be found anywhere. The short skirt did nothing more than partially cover her lap. She sat admiring the huge diamond in her wedding ring. A video game totally consumed two small children in the back seat.

An old gray Chevrolet forced itself in front of the Mercedes and immediately came to a stop. The attorney slammed on his brakes. The children dropped their video game to the floor. His wife grabbed the seat on both sides of her knees for support.

Before the wheels stopped turning a huge black man squirted some dirty water on the windshield and appeared to be wiping it off with the newspaper he held in his hand. He quickly positioned himself by the drivers' window so that the driver could see the shiny object concealed inside the newspaper.

A tall bald headed man came up on the passenger side, leaned down licking his lips and smiling at the drivers' wife. She could see the gun inside the newspaper pressed against her window. There was no way to cover those golden globes on her chest, so she tugged at the short skirt, remembering to keep her wedding ring concealed beneath her shapely legs.

The big man on the drivers' side extended his empty hand toward the driver and pointed the news paper at his chest. There was a smile on his huge face. The gap between his teeth was wide enough to see down his throat. The driver hesitated and the smile began to disappear. The driver shot a quick glance at the bald headed man eyeballing his wife. His confidence seemed to be failing him .He was obviously searching for an opportunity to drive out of this situation.

The car behind him began to honk the horn. Someone was yelling out of the window. The sound of metal tapping against the window brought him back to the reality of this situation. The big man had run out of patience. He extended his empty hand in the direction of the driver again. The newspaper now pointed directly at his head and the eyes of the big man said "do it now".

Reluctantly the driver rolled down his window and placed his wallet into the open hand. The two men quickly stepped away from the car. The old gray Chevrolet moved ahead far enough for the Mercedes to pass. The two men climbed into the back seat of the old Chevrolet and tossed their newspaper out of the window as the car turned the corner. I had observed the entire event from the bus stop. No one else seemed to notice.

As the Mercedes passed, the drivers' eyes made contact with mine. He looked me up and down as if he was mentally photographing me. I didn't know why and I didn't care. My feet hurt too much. A bus stopped and everyone except me got on. I didn't have enough money to ride a bus. I had only been using the bus stop as a place to rest. I stood up and willed my sore feet and tired legs to carry my aching body through the unfamiliar streets of down town Los Angeles.

SKID ROW

I stood on the corner of sixth and Crocker in the heart of skid row. My stomach growled loudly, demanding to know when I intended to eat again. I did not have an answer. I was reduced to tears as I took a closer look at my newest surroundings.

Shabby cardboard shelters lined one side of the street. Shopping carts filled with glass and cans were parked like limousines in front of and in between these shelters. Nervous looking, smelly, red eyed individuals mechanically went about their business. Misery was reflected in the absence of their smiles.

I slowly began to walk down Crocker toward Fifth Street. I was amazed at the activity taking place in broad day light. Across the street two well built young black men was mugging a small bald headed old Mexican. He was almost too drunk to stand up. He swung his wine bottle at the one closest to him and missed. The weight of the bottle made him run forward about three steps. A vicious, perfectly timed right cross put him down for the count.

The two men laughed as they stepped over him and crossed over to my side of the street. Two ladies of the night rushed over to the man lying face down in the street and quickly went through his pockets. He was out cold, still clinging to his precious bottle.

This entire area was a highly competitive market place of a special kind. Only a special kind of person could survive here. I began to feel like a gold fish that swam into an area where alligators gather at feeding time.

I knew that if I remained here, I too could end up face down in the street with strangers going through my pockets. Panic ripped through me like a run-a-way lightning bolt, erasing my last ounce of courage. I could smell the fear and feel the tension in the air. Desperation began to nip at my heels.

I armed myself with my meanest "Don't mess with me face" and forced myself to keep walking. If someone had sneezed I probably would not have been able to stop myself from running away.

I passed close to five men huddled together. Two of them watched me suspiciously as I approached. The shortest one in the group raised a glass pipe to his lips and fired it up. I was forgotten the first time he flicked his bic.

I turned the corner at fifth and Crocker and a truck pulled to the curb and began to pass out sandwiches and milk. I learned that you can inhale a sandwich so fast you hardly remember putting it into your mouth. Peanut butter and bologna had never tasted that good before. I leaned back against a telephone pole – tilted my head back and dumped a carton of milk down my throat.

Loud curse words erupted inside the cardboard shelter where the five men had been smoking. Someone screamed as a tall skinny man burst through the doorway at full speed, knocking down two people that tried to block the entrance. A single shot rang out and he lost control of his feet. His legs tangled and he fell in a pile ten feet in front of me.

People started running in every direction, yelling and pushing their carts in front of them. I stood there with my

George Mitchell

mouth open, hugging the telephone pole. I was glued to that spot.

A short man with a noticeable limp walked over to the fallen man and retrieved the glass pipe. The gun was still in his hands when he looked up at me. His eyes were shining like mirrors. I guess I needed a jump start.

He let out a blood curdling yell and the gun went off. I think my feet took off before I let go of that pole. The rest of my body caught up during my flight. I am not sure how long or how far I ran, but I do know that I ran pretty darn fast.

My heart was pounding like a jackhammer when I finally collapsed on a bench in the park. When I fully regained my composure I was forced to accept some undiluted facts.

I was broke. I looked bad and my feet hurt. I had made it all the way to the bottom and become a bum on skid row. I felt as though I had slid down a greased pole into a deep dark hole with all my hopes and dreams strapped to my back.

When you find yourself standing in a deep dark hole with your back against the wall it forces you to look up and remember the last place you saw the light. Somewhere up there is the light. Somewhere up there are hugs and kisses with my name on them. Somewhere out there is someone special that still care about me.

I had found that place in life where only two options were available to me. I could stay there and die, or find a way to climb out of that hole I was standing in. Skid Row was not an option for me. I refused to accept this place as home.

Refusing to accept Skid Row as my home was the first firm stand I had taken in a very long time. It made me feel really good.

I stood there like Clark Kent in a phone booth feeling myself being reborn. I wanted to burst out like superman and rescue myself. I knew that wasn't very realistic. I needed real help to climb out of this hole. I wasn't strong enough to do it by myself without falling again. Where could I possibly find the kind of help I needed?

Deep inside of me something stirred, and "I am somebody" just popped into my head. " Down but not out" was followed by "Yes I can ". Positive words and phrases began to flow through my brain like a river of hope. Perhaps I could find a way to use them as building blocks and construct a launch pad to the future.

I needed to find that one ingredient strong enough to hold them together forever. I was determined to build a strong foundation that would last. I needed something special—something everlasting. Where could I find one ingredient that strong?

My hand suddenly went deep into my pocket. It felt like someone else had jammed it in there. I jerked my hand out of my pocket and stared at it. I looked around to see if anyone noticed my strange behavior. When I didn't see anyone watching me, I opened my hand slowly. I was holding my last nickel. It was very tarnished but I could still read the words. "In God we trust". Could it be that simple? Could my belief in a higher power be the final ingredient?

My stomach had stopped growling and my aches and pains were ignored. I was beginning to rediscover traces of the old me. I didn't have a specific plan in mind or a special place to go. I simply squared my shoulders, put one sore foot in front of the other, stuck out my chest and walked away from Skid Row.

At seventh and Crocker I stopped and looked back. As I stood there an involuntary shiver rocked my body. If you can imagine running back and forth through a swarm of angry bees with your pants down without getting stung , you may have some idea what its like trying to survive on skid row.

It's possible to get mugged, raped, and even killed the same day and no one will care. With that frightening thought in mind I walked away from skid row, heading south on San Pedro. My destination didn't even matter. I was taking my first steps back to sanity holding a tarnished nickel in my hand. In addition to finding traces of the old me, I had found a positive way to use all of the panic and the pain.

DISCOVERY AND RECOVERY

I headed back to the area of Los Angeles that I was somewhat familiar with. I located a park with hot water and telephones. Perhaps if I was discrete enough I could call this place home until I put together a positive plan of action.

When the earth is your bed and the sky is the only roof over your head, priority number one automatically become survival. Priority number two has to be personal hygiene. When I was sure no one was looking I gave my left arm pit a quick sniff.

Wow! "What a rush". My eyes watered. It was not necessary to sniff anything else. Priority number two needed immediate attention. I washed myself, put on the cleanest of my dirty clothes, and began to figure out what I should do next.

I sat down at a picnic table and made a list of agencies that I thought could help me. The employment office seemed to be a good place to start. It was some distance away but if I started now I could get there before they closed. Ignoring the blisters on the bottom of my feet I was soon on the move again.

At the employment office I kept my arms pinned tightly to my sides. I felt that everyone else looked and smelled better than me. My name was called by a veterans' representative. He listened to my story with more than casual interest. He then informed me that less than three years ago he had stomped his glass pipe into tiny pieces and walked away from Skid Row.

He was very good at his job. It was obvious that he enjoyed helping people. Within minutes I had a list of agencies in the area that assisted homeless veterans with food, clothing and shelter. If I was going to get a room at the place he recommended I had to be there in forty five minutes. I could never walk that distance in forty five minutes

I accepted the fact that mother earth would probably be my bed again tonight. I rubbed my tarnished nickel as I stood up and extended my hand to thank him. He held my hand longer than I felt necessary. A question had begun to form in my mind when he pressed a twenty dollar bill into my palm.

"You have a bus to catch" was his last words to me. He picked up my file and walked away. I went to the bus stop thanking god for the man that remembered what it's like to be on skid row. I made myself a promise that some day I would do something special for him.

It was wonderful having a roof over my head again. My room had a bed, two chairs, a table, a small refrigerator and a television set. It was like having my own castle.

RECUPERATION AND PREPARATION

My feet looked like they had been micro waved and my right leg was badly swollen. Medication and elevation was prescribed to solve these problems. I spent two weeks recuperating, getting my wardrobe together and preparing a resume.

When I returned to the doctor for a follow-up he referred me to a social worker that specialized in helping veterans reach their full potential. He hung up the phone and told me to go right in. I walked into her office with my resume in my brief case and my tarnished nickel in my hand.

She reminded me of "Prissy the chicken" from my favorite cartoon show. The white bonnet was missing but all the other characteristics were in place. She had the same pale complexion, the thin pointed nose, and the extra thick lenses in her eye glasses. There was a soft sensitivity about her that made her appear fragile. I had my doubts about her.

I couldn't wait to impress her with the resume that I had worked on for two weeks. I whipped it out and placed it on the desk in front of her. I was positive this document would show her who I was and the potential I possessed. I didn't know it, but I was about to be surprised.

She finished reading, laid my paper on the desk, picked up a scratch pad and pointed at the door. "Go get yourself some lunch and come back in an hour".

She had begun to type before I reached the door. I put my tarnished nickel back into my pocket as I closed the door behind me. I was disappointed and believed this to be a complete waste of my time.

When I returned to her office she handed me a freshly typed document. "Read it" she demanded firmly. I could not believe what she had done to my resume. She had used the same information that I provided to describe a completely different person. Facts about me that I had thought to be unimportant were now primary information.

I had presented myself as being qualified to be a maintenance supervisor. This new document showed that I had the educational background, experience and expertise to organize and supervise a corporation.

My new opinion of her was one of deepest respect. My new opinion of myself was impossible to measure. She had recognized the desperation and determination that drove me and armed me with a document that would impress even the most skeptical employer.

She removed her glasses for the first time. I was surprised by the fire in her beady little eyes. Her aggressive stare nailed me to my seat. Her voice was hypnotic when she spoke these words: "The most precious jewels are not fully appreciated until someone makes them shine". "That's what I do for people." "You are a diamond in the rough" "I truly believe that you are destined to shine".

She stood up and extended her tiny little hand. I jumped to my feet jerking my hand out of my pocket. My tarnished nickel fell on her desk. She picked it up and looked at it curiously. She then said to me, "the best advice can be found in the strangest places". I left her office trying to remember when I had put my hand back into my pocket. On the bus I realized that I didn't even know her name.

George Mitchell

I read my new resume many times before climbing into bed. I really did have a lot of experience and expertise to offer a potential employer. My confidence began to grow. My imagination began to soar!!!

Unable to fall asleep, I turned on the television. There was a special on about a place called Chrysalis. They helped with resume preparation and distribution to potential employers. They also provided phones, job placement specialists, and related services that prepare applicants for interviews.

I wrote down the address and phone number and climbed into bed. Sleep would not come. I fumbled in the dark until I found my pants and fell asleep with my tarnished nickel in my hand. The bus traveled east on seventh street. I had an eerie feeling as I passed seventh and Crocker. That was where I had been standing when I took what I thought would be my last look at skid row.

CHRYSALIS

The Chrysalis house was near the corner of seventh and San Pedro. That was the last corner I turned as I walked away from skid row. Could there be some special reason I had to come back to skid row for help? I hoped the answer was no, but the question still remained in my head.

The people at Chrysalis were very professional. My resume was passed around like a treasure map. People peered over the top of wall dividers and poked their heads around corners to get a look at me. This made me feel kind of special.

I was escorted directly to a job placement specialist. There was a position available that my resume showed me to be qualified to perform. Two hotels had been converted into single family dwellings. The idea was to provide a safe environment for skid row dwellers desiring to stop their downward slide to the bottom. The search for the right person to help them regain their confidence and begin to set positive goals for themselves may be over. My resume had convinced them that I could be that person.

After a brief discussion I discarded the possibility. After all, these residential hotels were located in the heart of skid row. Dealing with skid row people required a special kind of person. I didn't even want to be here. As a matter of fact I couldn't wait to leave. I didn't mind helping someone that found the courage to walk away from skid row, but I had no intention of trying to stay here and be the person they were searching for.

I spent the next two weeks searching through want ads, making phone calls, and sending out resumes. Occasionally I was rewarded with an interview that left me feeling that I had just played the job lottery with absolutely no chance of winning.

Through casual conversation with another job searcher I learned that there was a residential hotel three blocks away. It was affordable and described as a great place to stay.

A week later I applied for residency with my resume in one hand and my tarnished nickel in the other. I was hired as part time maintenance man before the ink was dry. My compensation was a free room. I had hit the lottery.

I reported to work every day well groomed and eager to perform. I wore my tool belt low like a cowboy. I probably had the fastest hammer and screwdriver in the west.

Two weeks after I began working I was called into the office. The general manager and his two assistants were there. The general manager and one of his assistants were blue eyed blondes with strange accents. The third person was a chubby black man wearing make up. He licked his lips and smiled at me. Oversized lace panties and pink suspenders just popped into my mind.

When I was alone with the general manager, he laid a copy of my resume on his desk and asked me a few questions about my management and supervisory skills. When we finished discussing my military background he nodded his approval. I was then informed that a copy of my resume was in the possession of his boss. He was personally going to recommend that I be interviewed to be his replacement. He planned to return to England soon.

George Mitchell

Without knowing it, I had moved into and become a part time maintenance man at the very hotel that I was going to be interviewed to manage. I was about to walk through the door when he said, "I believe that you are the one we have been searching for".

Was it coincidence or destiny? I guess it didn't really matter. I would deal with that when it became the main issue. Meanwhile I had two towel racks to put up and a toilet to unplug.

PREPARATION

I had put myself in a unique position. In addition to information contained in my resume, performance reports from the present general manager would also have a lot of value. From now on I would be performing under a microscope. A part time job replacing light bulbs and unplugging toilets would never mean more to a potential employee.

I took it as a personal challenge and made it "show time". I seized every opportunity to showcase myself. This was reflected in my general appearance and job performance. I established an open door policy around the clock for anyone needing maintenance. My reputation as a reliable, dedicated individual earned me the respect of both tenants and management.

My confidence in my ability to be a general manager had grown tremendously. I knew every inch of the hotel and every tenant by name. I also knew about some illegal activity being conducted within the hotels. I had begun to believe that I was the one they had been searching for.

The director of operations gave me a history lesson while I waited to be interviewed.

The primary reason for converting these hotels into single family units was to give skid row dwellers a fighting chance at breaking the strangle hold of the row and working their way back into the main stream of society.

The second part of the plan had been to create programs within the buildings that focused on rebuilding self esteem and setting positive goals. The search for the right person to complete this project had always failed. Perhaps I was the one they had been searching for.

I stood there holding my tarnished nickel, well groomed and confident. Five different people observed closely as I answered their questions. Each question revolved around problems that already existed within the hotels. A variety of problem solving skills would be required to solve them. I knew that I possessed all of them.

The Hero of Skid Row

Living and working in the hotels had allowed me to observe from the tenants' point of view where management had failed them. I had personally observed management solving a tenant problem with a baseball bat. There was no respect for tenants or from tenants. I knew how to provide better solutions. My confidence surged and my mouth opened and told them that they would be doing themselves a favor if they hired me. That ended my interview.

There was silence in the room as I was escorted from the room. I had not intended to say that. I remember rubbing my tarnished nickel just before those words bounced off my brain and came out through my mouth. I had been as surprised as they were, but I didn't let it show. Something strange had just happened to me.

I returned to my part time job changing light bulbs, unplugging toilets, and fixing things. Interviews for the position continued, while I continued to be the best maintenance man in Los Angeles.

Many problems arise when you have pimps, pushers, prostitutes, felons, drug abusers and, Homosexuals living under the same roof. The person selected to solve these problems could not be a diamond in the rough. They had to shine!!!

I had applied for many jobs in the past that I thought I needed. This time I had applied for a job that needed me. I knew that I was the right person for the job, but my attitude during my interview may have sunk that ship.

A rumor spread through the hotel that I was going to be the new general manager, but it's hard to take a rumor of that magnitude seriously when you're walking around with a plunger in your hand.

Tenants began to bypass management and bring their problems to me. I must admit that it made me feel really good when a drug addict gave me his money to hold until morning so that he could pay his rent.

A week before Christmas the director of operations made it official and announced that I was to become the new general manager. I sat there reading my appointment letter and rubbing my tarnished nickel. I noticed that the tarnish was wearing off.

The present general manager had a week to train me. I surprised him by asking him to explain to me what I was expected to accomplish. I read the original plan and decided I did not even want to try it.

The following day I submitted my own written plan designed to accomplish the same goals. He was surprised and pleased that I would suggest these changes in strategy while I still had a plunger in one hand.

I had surprised him. Now it was his turn to surprise me. He informed me that he was one of the senior partners and would personally monitor my progress. If I did turn out to be the one they were looking for my bonus would be substantial.

"Is there anything else you want me to do before I give up this chair"? There was a hint of sarcasm in the way he said it. I didn't let that bother me. "Yes, you can take your assistants with you". "I don't want to work with them". "They can fill out applications if they want to remain as tenants." "I will find my own assistants and make changes as needed when I sit in that chair".

Monday morning found me sitting in that chair, spit shined and ready to perform. It was only 4:00 am, but I needed to observe some things prior to the scheduled meeting. The cleaning crew had made the office sparkle. I decided they were good enough to keep. They knew that I was watching them.

The security guards had to cover three floors in two buildings. They were required to pass my office every thirty minutes. They had not been seen in more than an hour. A tenant from the second hotel stopped by to tell me that the security guards were in the garage smoking chronic with a girl.

His name was Jon St.Francis. He was always well groomed and liked by the tenants that lived there. I had observed him helping people while I performed my duties as maintenance man. By the time our conversation ended he had agreed to be my assistant.

The meeting went well. Jon St-Francis was introduced as my assistant. The maintenance crew received compliments and both security guards were fired. Anyone desiring jobs as security guards or a part time maintenance man was encouraged to apply immediately. I made my position very clear.

1. Rules and regulations would be posted and enforced by me.
2. Everyone would become involved in making this a safer place to live.
3. All illegal activity taking place within the two hotels must cease immediately.

No one was singled out by name, but they knew who they were, and they knew that I knew who they were.

My authority had been established. My plan of action had successfully been set in motion. I left no doubt in anyone's mind that I was to be taken seriously.

My tool belt and plunger was passed on to the new maintenance man. My new security guards were posted. My first day as the new general manager had been completed.

I went to bed thinking about all the effort I had put into preparing myself to leave skid row. I remember thinking that after I left I would help someone else that found the courage to walk away. Why do I now feel that I belong here?

It feels as if god himself has rewritten this script, and made me the star. I was not destined to help those that walked away. I was destined to help those that stayed.

Instead of feeling frustrated I felt extremely confident, because if god rewrote the script and made me the star, he would also be my director. I fell asleep absolutely positive that I was the one they had been searching for.

Rent was collected and I went to the bank to make the deposit. While at the bank I became aware that someone was watching me. I could not remember where, but I had seen him before. He got out of line and walked out. I finished my business and walked out behind him. He was sitting in the drivers' seat of a gold trimmed black Mercedes parked at the curb.

I flashed back to the bus stop where we had made eye contact. I remember how he seemed to single me out as he drove away. I never expected to see him again, but there he was, mentally photographing me again.

Instead of driving away he went back into the bank. I returned to the hotel with hair standing up on the back of my neck. I could not resist looking over my shoulder before stepping inside.

I entered the hotel just as the mailman was locking the mail box. He pointed me out to two men. They looked like twins. They were dressed alike and wore matching no nonsense expressions on their faces. Their pictured identification declared them to be United States Treasury Agents.

My heart skipped a couple of beats when they told me they needed to discuss a very important matter with me. My brain went into overdrive searching for a possible reason. What did they think I had done?

I laid the mail on my desk and called my employers. They were already aware of their presence and told me to cooperate. I don't know what I expected them to say, but that wasn't it. I had a feeling they were going to spoil my day.

They instructed me to distribute the mail, and observed closely as I sorted the mail into seventy five individual mail slots with tenants names on them. Mail with names that I did not recognize was dropped into a box beneath the mail slots and stamped "not at this address". "Return to sender". There was a total of 21 pieces of mail to be returned. 15 of them were U S Treasury checks.

They compared the names on the checks to a printed copy that they had brought with them. They nodded their heads in agreement and returned the checks to me. One of them accompanied me to the mailbox and observed as I locked it. I gave them the records showing all the people that lived in the hotels in the past four years.

I announced over the intercom that mail could now be picked up. No one was allowed to pick up anyone else's mail. Within twenty five minutes all mail had been distributed and I turned my attention back to the two men.

They had to go back three years to find the last name on their list. They had written down the move in and move out dates for each person. The word "deceased" was written beside three of the names.

Suddenly things started to make sense. These guys were on a mission. They were tying up loose ends and I was helping them do that. They had a plan and it was coming together. I began to feel like a secret agent. I felt six inches taller as we walked to the mailbox together.

I was the only one surprised to find it empty. One of them opened the door and instructed a police officer to stand outside. The other one spoke into his 2-way radio. I was still trying to figure out what happened to the mail.

I was instructed to clear the area and wait in the office. The two of them took the elevator to the lower level. Their expressions indicated they were in no mood to be challenged. From the office I watched the elevator door like a little kid waiting for Santa Clause.

The elevator door opened and the three of them stepped into the lobby. His hands were cuffed behind his back. The make up was slightly smeared. The smile had disappeared from his face, but he couldn't seem to stop licking his lips. Oversized lace panties and pink suspenders popped into my head again.

One of the agents came over and showed me the names on the checks in his hand. I signed a statement that these were the same checks I had locked in the mailbox. The agent that had witnessed me locking them in there would later sign the same statement. A good bye and a hand shake later it was over, but I still felt like a secret agent. They had made my day!!

The director of operations informed me that an attorney had been asking personal questions about me. I couldn't imagine why I was attracting so much attention. I didn't even know any lawyers in Los Angeles. I certainly hadn't done anything worth investigating. If he was any good he would discover that for himself.

I shrugged it off as being important and turned my attention to making my hotels the best they could be. The tenants bought into my philosophy and rallied to support my agenda.

Every community has busy bodies that know everyone else's business. We had them scattered throughout the hotels on every level. I had an idea that would make them famous. They were all invited to come to my office at the same time.

They loved the challenge I presented to them, and united to form "The Nosey Neighbors' Club". My interior security force had been formed. They would document all inappropriate behavior on their floors and give it to me. Another part of my plan had come together.

Signs were posted throughout the buildings saying: "Respect your neighborhood"- "Respect yourself" and " The nosey neighbors are watching you". Security guards were eliminated and the $300.00 a week that had been budgeted to pay them was used to start a recreation / entertainment fund. Mr. St-James was appointed treasurer and a planning committee was selected to work with him. Another step had been taken to show tenants how to work together.

Ideas began to flow like poetry in motion. Leaders began to separate themselves from followers. Everyone became involved in programs that they themselves suggested to rebuild confidence and self esteem. Everything had to meet with my approval before it was implemented. We rapidly became the standard of excellence used to evaluate other residential hotels.

I started to get calls about available hotel management opportunities throughout the city. I never told anyone about the calls. Occasionally the director of operations or one of the managers would escort some official looking men through the buildings. I really wasn't very concerned because my buildings were always immaculate.

I had achieved every goal included in my written plan at the time of my hiring. "The Nosy Neighbors' Club" had proven to be a very effective interior security force. All expectations had been surpassed, and our waiting list was growing longer every day. My entire plan had come together.

Space became available when two tenants were evicted. The vacancies were filled by my assistant while I attended a Meeting with the owners. What a meeting that turned out to be!

Six men including the general manager that I had replaced waited for me in the conference room. Together they formed a group of investors involved in converting skid row hotels into facilities just like the two I managed, in five different states. They needed a man that could go to each facility and bring them up to the standards I had established here. This was not an interview. This was a job offer.

I had been observed by all of them from the time I announced that they would be doing themselves a favor if they hired me. There was something about that kind of attitude that got their attention and convinced them that I just might be the one.

The prestige, money and respect would have been enough, but when they threw in the automobile of my choice I quickly accepted the offer. They gave me thirty days to complete my exit strategy which included finding my own replacement.

My replacement must be someone capable of maintaining what I had established. I knew exactly where to find that person, and looked forward to keeping a promise.

As I walked back to the hotel I thanked god for rewriting the script and making me the star.

The two newest tenants had just signed their rental agreements and picked up their keys from St-James when I entered the hotel. They looked at me strangely as they walked past me. My expression must have closely resembled someone that had just seen a ghost.

I had flashed back to the time I saw them standing beside the gold trimmed black Mercedes with newspapers in their hands. I am not sure why I felt it necessary, but I pulled their files, checked their pictured ID's and committed their names to memory.

THE ATTORNEY

He stepped out of the parked car and met me at entrance to the bank. He identified himself as an attorney. He needed my help. Our conversation once again transported me back to that bus stop where I sat watching a robbery in progress.

He handed me an envelope containing three sketches. Two of them were the faces of the robbers. The third was a picture of me. My facial expression confirmed that I had been a witness. I finally understood why he focused on me as he drove away.

I could feel the excitement building as he filled in the blanks. God blessed him with a photographic memory. He was also an artist. Several police reports described the same two robbers. They had been seen in this area on several occasions. He was positive I knew what they looked like. I was asked to notify him if I saw them. He wanted the satisfaction of pointing them out to the police. I just wanted them out of my building. Perhaps we could both get what we wanted.

I didn't have a photographic memory but I did remember the names. I wrote the name and address beneath the face on the each sketch and gave them back to him. I decided to keep the sketch of myself. It really was very good. It was my turn to fill in the blanks.

"No", I did not want to be a witness in court. [The others that had been robbed could be witnesses.] "Yes", I would accept his offer to represent me free of charge if I needed him, and "No" I never intended to rest at another bus stop.

THE PROMISE

I approached the table where he was having his lunch. There was no file or telephone near him but, he appeared totally organized. He looked at me curiously at first, then his face lit up as total recognition came to him. He stood up, pumped my hand vigorously, and voiced his approval. I told him I was here to keep a promise that I made the day he went beyond the boundaries of his job to help me.

There was surprise and pleasure at what I offered him. He looked forward to the challenge and thanked me for choosing him. We agreed on a training schedule and he was putting his two week notice in writing as I left him.

I arrived back at the hotel just in time to see Baldy and Hefty being escorted from my building. The gold trimmed black

Mercedes was parked directly across the street. The driver waved to me and huge smiles were exchanged between us. This had been a good day.

The director of operations was pleased with my replacement choice. St-James already knew him from the employment office. They would work well together.

My work here was almost done. One week from today I would receive the keys to my new car, pick up my bonus check, and move on to one of my five new assignments. I checked all of my pockets but never found my nickel again.

If you find yourself on skid row someday with a tarnished nickel in your hand, read it before you spend it. The message on the coin is priceless.

With my bonus check in my pocket I watched Los Angeles disappear in the rearview mirror of my new gold trimmed black Mercedes. It was like taking a piece of skid row with me, but I didn't mind. I didn't mind at all.